ANIMALS
at WORK

Horses
at Work

Julia Barnes

GARETH**STEVENS**,INC.

A Member of the WRC Media Family of Companies

Please visit our Web site at: www.garethstevens.com
For a free color catalog describing Gareth Stevens Publishing's list of high-quality books and multimedia programs, call 1-800-542-2595 (USA) or 1-800-387-3178 (Canada). Gareth Stevens Publishing's fax: (414) 332-3567.

Library of Congress Cataloging-in-Publication Data

Barnes, Julia, 1955-
    Horses at work / Julia Barnes.— North American ed.
        p. cm. — (Animals at work)
    Includes bibliographical references and index.
    ISBN 0-8368-6225-2 (lib. bdg.)
    1. Horses—Juvenile literature. 3. Working animals—Juvenile literature. I. Title.
SF302.B38 2006
636.1'0886—dc22   2005054066

This North American edition first published in 2006 by
Gareth Stevens Publishing
A Member of the WRC Media Family of Companies
330 West Olive Street, Suite 100
Milwaukee, WI 53212 USA

This U.S. edition copyright © 2006 by Gareth Stevens, Inc. Original edition copyright © 2005
by Westline Publishing, The Warren, Aylburton, Lydney, Gloucestershire, GL15 6DX.

Gareth Stevens editor: Carol Ryback
Gareth Stevens designer: Charlie Dahl

Photo Credits:
M.K. Snowhite: 1, 24. Michael and Nancy Kerson, Mustangs 4 Us, http://www.mustangs4us.com/: 5.
Defence Animal Centre: 11. © Dori Luzbetak 2003; provided by Fred Klink, 11th U.S. Cavalry,
Commemorative: 12. First Company Governor's Horse Guards of Connecticut: 13. Norbert Woehnl: 16.
Tony Ding and Bob Hunt: 18. Alan Hiscox, © Metropolitan Police Service Mounted Branch: 17. Eva Leitinger,
Spanish Riding School: 21. Loita Karen Anderson: 25. Riding for the Disabled Association: 26, 27. Verity Lea
and Tony Miller, Equestrian Theatre Limited: 28, 29.

Printed in the United States of America

1 2 3 4 5 6 7 8 9 10 09 08 07 06

Contents

Introduction

Wild horses have run free on open grasslands for thousands of years, on constant alert for **predators**, and moving on when food was scarce. They developed the skills they needed in order to survive: speed, strength, stamina, and lightning-fast reactions — and these traits are what make the horse so useful.

Over time, people have created a special relationship with the horse, working in partnership with an animal that still retains many wild **instincts**. Humans found a way to understand the horse and to use its abilities so it can perform an amazing number of different tasks. Meet:

- big, heavy horses that can pull huge loads.
- **agile** horses, used for rounding up cattle.
- super-fast horses that are trained to race.
- well-trained police horses, used to control riots.
- circus horses that perform amazing tricks.
- horses that provide therapy for riders with disabilities.

Discover how working horses are trained and learn about the wonderful — and often lifelong — partnerships between horse and humans that result.

A team of Belgian workhorses plow a farm in California.

The First Horses

Coming in from the wild

The human relationship with horses began in ancient times. Horses were at first hunted for meat, but humans soon found a better use for these wild animals.

The first wild horses lived in Central Asia. Over the centuries, humans **domesticated** these animals and used them for herding cattle, transporting heavy loads pulling wagons, and going into battle.

Horses on board

Christopher Columbus brought horses along on his second voyage to the West Indies in 1493. It was the first time Native peoples had seen such animals.

Over the next few decades, other European explorers and settlers brought more horses with them. People and horses evenutally made their way into the North and South American continents.

At some point, a few horses managed to excape from their human owners. These wild horses grew into herds of hardy, interbred horses called **mustangs** that fed on the rich prairie grasses of the Great Plains.

Native Americans tamed some of these animals, using them for transportation, in battle, and as objects for trading. Horses were a symbol of wealth and status.

In some instances when an important Native American war leader died, his favorite horses were sacrificed so they could accompany him to the next life.

Herds of wild mustangs roam free in some areas of North America.

On the Ranch

The pace, skill, and agility of cowboy horses

Early settlers on the cattle ranches in North America lived tough lives. Horses often provided the only means of travel across the huge distances and the only way to control the cattle. Cowboys used horses to herd, rope, and pen the livestock. For this, they needed a horse with exceptional abilities.

The ideal horse

Cowboys wanted a horse that they could not only ride all day, but also could, when required, produce a burst of speed. They needed an agile, obedient horse that could twist and turn, and willingly ran alongside **steers**.

The quarter horse, now the world's most popular breed, was developed in the 1600s by settlers on the East Coast of North America. They bred imported horses with the tough, versatile horses used by Native Americans. Their breeding efforts produced a strong, compact, muscular horse that worked on farms and plantations.

Horses help their owners rope cattle.

Cattle branding is a routine job on a ranch.

When not working, the owners sometimes raced their horses in fast and furious quarter-mile dashes. These animals became known as "quarter horses" for their amazing sprinting ability. These horses could go from a standing start to about 40 miles (65 kilometers) per hour in a single stride.

As the pioneers moved westward in the 1800s and opened up cattle ranches, they took the quarter horses with them. The agility, strength, and ability of the quarter horses to work with cattle soon became legendary.

Multi-talented

Horses that herd cows learn a variety of skills. These range from herding and driving cattle over long distances to the other ranching tasks, such as coralling cattle for branding or separating certain cows from the main herd.

Some ranches now specialize in vacations where tourists learn how to ride a cow-herding horse and get a firsthand experience of life on a ranch.

DID YOU KNOW
A quarter horse can cover a distance of 0.25 miles (0.40 km) in about twenty-one seconds.

Pulling Power

Gentle giants of the horse world

Draft horses are bred for their size and their incredible strength. These animals have an easy-going, laid-back nature that suits their steady pace.

On the farm
Before the **Industrial Revolution** in the nineteenth century, all the work carried out on farms relied on **horsepower**.

Hefty draft horses were harnessed to the plow, and worked long, hard days in the fields. When not used for **plowing**, they pulled wagons burdened with farm produce to market.

Belgian horses pull a hay wagon for Amish farmers in Ohio.

Different breeds of draft horses, such as Belgians, shires, Suffolk punches, Percherons, and Clydesdales were developed in countries throughout Europe, including in England, France, and Belgium.

The first European draft horses were imported to the United States in the late 1830s. By 1900, about twenty-seven thousand purebred draft horses were working on U.S. farms. Farmers often cross-bred their draft horses with smaller horses. These breeds proved invaluable for pulling heavy loads for the railroads that were being constructed across the country.

Fighting for survival
With the introduction of tractors and other

Shire horses take on a new role as show animals in parades.

gas-powered machines, in the 1920s, draft horses were no longer needed, and their numbers fell so dramatically that these magnificent horses nearly died out. In the 1960s, only about two thousand shire horses were left in the world. In 1966, only nine Suffolk punch **foals** were born.

Fortunately, horse enthusiasts worked hard to keep the **bloodlines** of the draft breeds going. Today, some are still used in their traditional role on farms. The **Amish** communities in the United States rely on Belgians and Percherons to plow the land. Draft horses also create a spectacular sight pulling brewers' **drays** through cities, as they appear in shows and parades. They also compete in plowing matches. The largest brewery in the United States currently has a touring Clydesdale team that performs in parades and at festivals and other events across the nation.

> **DID YOU KNOW**
> The "horsepower" rating of modern engines measures how many horses it would take to produce that same amount of power.

Heroic Horses

Fearless mounts used in wartime

One of the earliest recorded uses of horses in war was General Hannibal of Carthage's crossing of the Alps with his army in 218 B.C. Hannibal planned to invade Rome and set off on the five-month trek with twenty thousand foot soldiers, six thousand mounted (soldiers on horseback, called the **cavalry**), and thirty-eight elephants.

Into battle

When Julius Caesar was expanding the Roman Empire, in about 50 to 55 B.C., he needed horses that could pull huge wagons piled high with equipment. The **native** heavy horses that lived in Belgium and northern France were perfect for the job. Later, Napoleon, who ruled France in the early nineteenth century, used the same strong, tough breeds, as well as smaller horses that were ridden into battle, in his army.

Cavalry troops often led the charge into battle.

In certain areas of rough terrain, an army uses horses to carry supplies.

Cavalry charge

When guns and **artillery** became the weapons of war, horses were needed in two ways. Draft horses pulled the artillery, and the smaller, more agile horses, known as the cavalry, were ridden into battle. Cavalry horses had to endure gunfire and explosives at close quarters in the midst of a battle. Sadly, many horses were wounded or killed.

Throughout the world, horses played a vital role in warfare, and they participated in the most famous battles in history. The last time large numbers of horses were used in battle was in World War I (1914–1918). With the invention of tanks and other weaponry, the role of horses in warfare was largely at an end.

New role

The military still call on the horse's services, but no longer in battle. When a natural disaster, such as an earthquake, occurs, getting supplies to an area becomes extremely important. Many military units now use packhorses to carry heavy weights over rough terrain when a natural disaster destroys or damages road and railroads.

> ### DID YOU KNOW
> Napoleon's favorite horse was a gray Arabian called *Marengo*. The horse was wounded on several occasions. Marengo had five scars. A bullet lodged at the top of his tail.

Ceremonial Horses

The pride of the regiment on parade

Fortunately, horses are no longer ridden into battle, but they still play a role in ceremonial occasions. The United States Cavalry remembers its brave and victorious history, and cavalry horses are a great attraction when major parades are staged.

On parade

The history of the First Company Governor's Horse Guards, based in Avon, Connecticut, goes back to 1788, when veterans of the American Revolution formed a mounted guard to honor the governor and other

Memories of the cavalry remain fresh when horses are used in parades and other public events.

The First Company Governor's Horse Guards of Connecticut marched in President Dwight D. Eisenhower's inaugural parade in 1957.

important visitors to the state.

The Horse Guards have continued performing this ceremonial role over the centuries, and play an important role in national events, such as the inauguration parade of President Eisenhower in 1957.

Mounted units traditionally take part in inauguration parades. At President George W. Bush's 2005 inauguration, riders and horses from the Caisson Platoon and the 1st Armored Cavalry Division honored the president.

Under fire

The horses of the Royal Artillery in England are also in popular demand. Horses are selected and trained to pull artillery — just as they did when they went into battle. Now, however, these skills thrill crowds at public demonstrations and perform for many types of official occasions.

The strong artillery horses pull heavy cannons at **canter** — a smooth, steady speed that is just less than a gallop — and then stand completely still while the cannons are fired. The noise is deafening, but these horses — like the horses used for battle — have learned to stay calm under fire.

Funeral march

Black horses, such as Friesians, make a spectacular sight in official funeral processions. When a U.S. president dies, the long funeral procession traditionally includes a riderless horse with boots stuck backwards in the stirrups. The position of the boots symbolizes a leader's last look at his troops.

Born To Race

The fastest horses on Earth

The thoroughbred is the fastest and most valuable of all the horse breeds. It was developed for one reason — to race. Champion racehorses are worth millions of dollars.

Royal patrons

In the 1700s, the British royal family started to breed racing horses, using a mixture of breeds from Spain, Italy, Ireland, and Scotland. Later, three Oriental **stallions** were imported and bred with local racing horses. This was the birth of the thoroughbred breed. The bloodline of every modern **thoroughbred** now alive is linked to these three stallions.

Racing power

A thoroughbred is so fast because it is bred for speed. Its body is lean and fine-boned, combining athleticism and strength. Its deep chest allows for plenty of room for lung expansion, and its long stride covers a lot of ground and gives the horse a maximum forward push for all-out galloping.

Racehorses start their careers at a very young age. Most enter training at about age two, and will run their first races that season. The races with the biggest prize money, such as the Kentucky Derby in the

Horse racing has been a popular spectator sport in the United States for well over a century.

Ready to run: Horses line up in the starting stalls before a big race.

United States and the Epsom Derby in England are run by three-year-old horses.

Top races

Horse racing in the United States dates back to the late eighteenth century.

The famous Kentucky Derby was run for the first time in 1875 at Churchill Downs in Louisville. A colt named *Aristides* won.

The Kentucky Derby track is 1.25 miles (2 km) long. It occurs on the first Saturday in May. The Kentucky Derby is the first leg of the Triple Crown, a grueling schedule of three races in five weeks, in which the top three-year-old race-horses compete.

The second leg of the Triple Crown is the Preakness Stakes, held two weeks after the Derby at Pimlico Race Track in Baltimore, Maryland. Stage three is the Belmont Stakes, which is run at Elmont, New York.

Only eleven horses in history have ever won the Triple Crown. The twentieth century's last Triple Crown winner was named *Affirmed*. He took top honors in 1978.

Police Horses

Helping fight crime and keep the peace

Most police officers drive a squad car to the scene of a crime. For some police work, however, a horse is a better choice of transportation. Modern police departments all over the globe rely on some mounted officers to perform daily police duties.

Fighting crime

Policemen in London, England, first used horses in 1760 to catch criminals who stopped carriages and stole valuables from travelers. The success of the early horse and rider police teams led to the formation of more teams of mounted policemen. The mounted branch has remained a vital part of London's metropolitan police force ever since. Other police forces in England and in different countries soon followed their example.

In the United States in the nineteenth century,

Police officers on horses in New York City maneuver through traffic jams much easier than officers in squad cars.

Police horses are called on in many different situations. Crowd control is a regular part of their work.

as the pioneers moved westward, sheriffs kept order and fought crime. They often worked in remote settlements, and getting around without a horse would have been nearly impossible. Today, mounted police forces throughout the United States and Canada play an important role in law enforcement.

A modern role

Police horses are used in a number of ways, including:

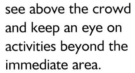

- *On patrol:* Mounted police **patrol** crowded areas to help reduce crimes such as robberies, vandalism, or auto theft.
- *Keeping order:* Police on horseback can control large crowds more easily. A police officer on a horse can see above the crowd and keep an eye on activities beyond the immediate area.
- *Sporting events:* Certain sporting events attract huge numbers of spectators. Occasionally, fights break out between **rival fans**. Police horses help patrol the crowds as the spectators come or leave an event.
- *Demonstrations:* When groups meet for a protest march, police horses are one of the best ways to keep them on the approved route. If the demonstrators become violent, police horses face the danger of injury from airborne objects and other forms of attack. In that case, the police on the horses use riot gear to control the crowd and provide protection.

In East Lansing, Michigan, a basketball game on April 2, 2005 erupted into a riot when the home team lost. Mounted police used pepper spray to disperse about two thousand angry fans. © Tony Ding Photography

In training

It takes a very special horse to cope with police work. The horse must be bold and obedient, with the temperament to work in demanding situations. In the United States, the quarter horse and the Morgan breeds are often used. In England, a thoroughbred mixed with one of the heavier draft breeds makes an excellent police horse.

Horse training varies depending on where the animal will work, but it follows roughly the same stages:

- *Stage One:* An instructor teaches the horse basic exercises in an arena on a long lead.

- *Stage Two:* The horse works with a rider in an enclosed, indoor school. Taped recordings of traffic, trains, and crowds are played so the horse gets used to real-life working conditions.

- *Stage Three:* Horse and rider go out into the open and practice special

Police horse training may include jumping through a hoop of fire. Such training teaches the horse to obey its rider, even when confronted with a dangerous situation.

exercises, such as how to move through a crowd. At this final stage of training, the horse is tested for its behavior in public.

All police horses are ridden by police officers who also go through intensive training. As well as riding the horse on patrol, the police officer is responsible for caring for the horse. The bond between horse and rider must become strong, because the team will often face frightening and dangerous situations in the line of duty.

Public displays

Promoting good public relations is an important part of police work, and many departments hold special events to show off their animals and promote goodwill among the public.

DID YOU KNOW

In a large crowd, a mounted police officer is as effective as twelve police officers walking through the crowd on foot. Mounted officers can see trouble spots at a distance because they sit so high over the crowd.

Dancing Horses

The dazzling skills of the Lipizzaner stallions

It takes many years to train a Lipizzaner stallion at the Spanish Riding School.

The stunning white horses of the Spanish Riding School prove that horses really can dance. The world-famous Lipizzaner stallions are trained to perform a horse ballet to music in the splendid surroundings of the Imperial Palace in Vienna, Austria.

Spanish Riding School

The white horses of the Spanish Riding School have drawn packed audiences since the seventeenth century, and today they are more popular than ever. These amazing horses and their highly skilled riders go on worldwide tours to show off their special riding skills.

Classical art

The **high school** style of riding is based on feats performed by

A capriole is one of the most dramatic moves performed by the Lipizzaner stallions.

the ancient Greeks. It takes many years for both rider and horse to perfect.

Lipizzaner horses are born dark and become lighter as they mature. They start their training when they are about four years old. A young horse is always matched with an experienced rider, who teaches the animal the many complicated moves.

The Lipizzaners

In 1850, a shipment of thirty-three purebred Andalusian horses were

sent from Spain to the Imperial Austrian stud farm in Lipizza (now Croatia). The offspring became the breeding stock for the Spanish Riding School. These highly trained horses became so famous that they were recognized as a breed in their own right — the Lipizzaners.

Great escape

The Lipizzaner stud farm has some of the most valuable breeding stock in the world. During World War II (1939–1945), however,

these precious animals were nearly lost. German forces took over the stud farm until U.S. and British forces regained control of it.

Tempel Farm

In 1958, Tempel and Esther Smith imported twenty Lipizzaners to the United States. Horses from the world-famous Tempel Farm in Wadsworth, Illinois, make up the finest bloodline outside of Europe. They perform at many ceremonies and special events.

Horse-drawn Transportation

Traveling through the ages

Imagine living in a city without cars, trucks, trains, or buses. The only means of getting around is on horseback or by riding in a horse-drawn carriage or wagon. That was what it was like one hundred fifty years ago. It might sound peaceful compared with the frantic traffic noise of a modern city. But, in fact, the roads were busy and bustling as horse-drawn carts and wagons, laden with produce, tried to overtake each other, grinding through the mud of dirt tracks.

Looking back

Only the wealthy could afford their own horse-drawn transportation. Most people relied on public transportation. As U.S. cities grew bigger in the mid-nineteenth century, public transportation lines using horses appeared, and by 1886, more than one hundred thousand horses and **mules** were used in hundreds of cities across the nation.

Although horses were used for moving people around, they also came in handy for moving goods from place to place. In the early twentieth century, horse-drawn milk, junk, and ice wagons were a common sight in cities.

A horse-drawn carriage pulls tourists in Dallas, Texas.

Competition is fast and furious in carriage driving trials.

Changing times

From the 1920s onward, the horse was gradually replaced by motorized cabs, electric street cars, and subways. New gasoline-powered trucks soon took over the job of transporting and delivering goods. The horse, once so important to city life, was no longer needed.

A new age

Fortunately, the role of horse-drawn transportation has not been lost. The popularity of using horse-drawn carriages for weddings and funerals is growing, and some businesses use horse-drawn carriages for publicity purposes. A number of cities also provide horse-drawn wagons and carriages for pleasure rides.

The skills required for carriage driving are also flourishing. Hackney Driving Championships and Carriage Driving Trials are fiercely contested sports with a worldwide following.

Sports Horses

The world of competition demands skill and courage

Horse enthusiasts have invented a wide range of sports requiring skill and dedication. Other horse sports demand a fair degree of courage.

Most horse sports are leisure activities, but some involve strong competitions. These finely tuned horse athletes perform to the best of their potential.

Rodeo sports

Rodeo sports, such as reining (showing off the horse's paces, including sensational spins and sliding stops), roping (lassoing steers on horseback), and cutting (separating a cow from the herd), are more popular than ever, with big money at stake.

Barrel racing

Barrel racing is a timed event designed for cowgirls and their horses. Horses enter the arena at full speed, steer around the barrels, and then exit. A rider loses points if she knocks over a barrel.

Chuckwagon racing

This sport dates back to the Wild West when chuckwagons — the cowboys' food wagon and cafeteria — would race between campsites.

Horses show off their skills, such as this sliding stop, at rodeos.

Chuckwagon racing is intensely competitive.

A fast barrel race lasts just under ten seconds.

Chuckwagon racing is fast and furious. As teams race against each other, they often reach speeds of 30 miles (48 km) per hour.

The chuckwagon race courses may include sharp turns.

DID YOU KNOW

A prize-winning barrel-racing horse is an expensive animal.

Riders With Disabilites

Horses that provide a special kind of freedom

Horses are still used for many traditional jobs, but new ways of working with them are still being developed. Specially trained horses used for different kinds of **therapy** are proving of enormous benefit to people with disabilities.

Charities
Charities in many parts of the world, have helped establish organizations that focus on helping people with disabilities ride horses or drive carriages. People of all ages, from young children through to adults, can take part. One such organization currently caters for riders age two to eighty! People with different disabilities, including those who need wheelchairs, the blind, or people with learning disabilities, can participate.

The horses
Trainers look for horses with the best **temperament** when they choose horses to train as therapy animals. The horses must be calm, quiet, and reliable. The instructors work with the horses to develop steady paces.

Horses and ponies are led at a steady pace so riders can enjoy a country trail.

A young rider takes a closer look at a therapy horse.

They also train the horses to accept riders who may have difficultly balancing. In some cases, the horses may wear special **tack**, such as a saddle with a handgrip, so that the rider feels safer.

The volunteers

All riders need help as they learn to ride, and some may require extra assistance. Volunteers lead the horses. They skillfully control the horses and offer advice and encouragement. The riding staff work closely with **physical therapists** and other health professionals so they know exactly how to help each rider.

The benefits

People with disabilities gain enormous benefits from horseback riding.

Riding a horse not only gives a sense of freedom and boosts self-confidence, but also helps the rider physically. The rider must work at keeping his or her balance, and this strengthens muscles throughout the body. Horseback riding also improves the general fitness of a person with disabilities.

DID YOU KNOW

Therapists are developing new ways to help children who are in trouble because of bad behavior. Caring for a horse and learning to ride helps these children learn a new sense of responsibility.

Circus Horses

Displays designed to thrill the crowds

For hundreds of years, horses have been star performers in the circus. Their beauty, athleticism, and skill thrills the crowds.

All over the world, a number of circuses specialize in spectacular performances where highly trained horses show off their remarkable talents. Many different breeds are used, but Arabs, Spanish horses and Cossacks are among the most popular.

Circuses follow strict guidelines that put the horses' health and safety first. Stabling and exercise areas are set up at every new location, and traveling is kept to a minimum to keep the horses from becoming too stressed or tired.

Courageous Cossacks

The fiery Cossack warriors from southern Russia needed horses that were fast, strong, agile, and fearless. The Cossack horses they bred met that challenge. The daring feats of Cossack riders were legendary, and the Cossack regiments were the most feared — and admired — of all the units in the Russian army.

Today, the Cossack's fighting past is a distant memory, but the amazing skills of the Cossack horses and riders, such as death hangs — where the rider hangs upside

The Cossacks put on a breathtaking display of speed and stunts.

© Equestrian Theatre

DID YOU KNOW
Many circus horses are trained using a clicker — a small metal box with a "tongue" that clicks when pressed. The horse learns to properly perform certain movements when it hears a click — and knows that a reward will follow.

Riders of Spanish horses in circuses often carry long wooden poles called *garrochas*. The poles were used for rounding up cattle. A rider needs great skill to carry his garrocha while controling his horse.

down, and double vaults — where the rider jumps on and off the horse as it canters, are performed by troupes of Cossacks in shows worldwide.

Amazing Arabs
The Arabian horse is the oldest and purest breed in the world, with records dating back to 300 B.C. This desert horse was tamed by the Bedouin peoples of North Africa and has worked with humans for many centuries.

The Arabian's stunning beauty makes it a natural choice for the circus, and these intelligent animals are trained to perform spectacular routines that show off their natural grace and elegance — and their remarkable obedience.

Spanish style
The Spanish Andalusian and the Portuguese Lusitana breeds are proud, spirited, and highly prized horses. Fast and agile, they were used in close-combat battles, in bullfighting arenas, and for rounding up cattle. These horses display their skills, including exciting **duels**, high school work (see *page 20*), and riding in formation in circuses around the world.

Glossary

agile: able to bend and move easily.

Amish: a religious community that rejects modern machinery.

artillery: large guns, such as cannons.

bloodlines: related animals; families.

canter: a rhythmic, rocking pace performed by a horse — faster than trotting, but slower than galloping.

cavalry: soldiers on horseback.

domesticated: animals that have been bred by man to live or work alongside humans.

drays: heavy wagons without sides.

duel: a fight between two enemies.

foals: young horses.

high school: a type of riding where the horse shows off its paces and performs special moves.

horsepower: a unit that measures the energy one horse produces.

Industrial Revolution: the mid-nineteenth century period of rapid development of machinery, railroads, and other powerful inventions.

instincts: the natural behavior of an animal.

mules: the offspring from matings of donkeys and horses.

mustangs: wild horses that roamed free and bred over several centuries in the western U.S.; mustangs were popular with Native Americans.

native: originating in that place.

patrol: a regular tour made of a place in order to guard it and keep order.

physical therapists: medical personnel who use physical actions (e.g., exercise and massage), instead of medication, to treat medical problems.

plowing: digging up soil to get it ready for planting crops.

predators: hunters.

purebred: an unmixed bloodline.

rival fans: fans from opposing teams.

rodeo: a competition or display of cowboy skills.

stallions: male horses used for breeding.

steers: young bulls.

tack: general name for the equipment used for riding horses.

temperament: character or personality.

therapy: treatment for a disease or disorder.

thoroughbred: animals from a pure bloodline.

traditional role: the common, accepted use of an animal or object.

Find Out More . . .

More books to read

Barnes, Julia. *101 Facts About Horses and Ponies*. *101 Facts About Pets* (series). Gareth Stevens (2001).

Boldt, Betty. *Dressage*. *The Horse Library* (series). Chelsea House (2001).

Budd, Jackie. *Horse & Pony Breeds*. *The Complete Guides to Horses and Ponies*. Gareth Stevens (1998).

Clutton-Brock, Juliet. *Horse*. DK Publishing (2000).

Dubowski, Mark. *A Horse Named Seabiscuit*. *All Aboard Reading*. *Station Stop 3*. (series). Grosset & Dunlap (2003).

Web sites

www.horses4kids.com/
Play games, solve puzzles, take a quiz on horses and more.

www.nps.gov/uspp/fhorsepage.htm
Learn about the United States Park Police Horse Mounted Unit.

www.pbs.org/wildhorses/
Discover the history of the wild mustangs of North America.

www.pbs.org/wnet/nature/mongolia/race.html
Answer questions about Mongolia to win a horse race across the Steppes.

www.ansi.okstate.edu/breeds/horses/
Click on specific horse breeds to learn more.

Index